CATNIP
selecting and training your cat

CATNIP
selecting and training your cat

by
Kurt Unkelbach

Illustrations by Haris Petie

Prentice-Hall, Inc.
Englewood Cliffs, New Jersey

To Betsy and Billy Carr

CATNIP   Selecting and Training Your Cat
by Kurt Unkelbach
© 1970 by Kurt Unkelbach
Illustrations © 1970 by Prentice-Hall, Inc.
Library of Congress Catalog Card Number: 79-102655*
Printed in the United States of America • *J*
13-121095-5
Prentice-Hall International, Inc., London
Prentice-Hall of Australia, Pty. Ltd., Sydney
Prentice-Hall of Canada, Ltd., Toronto
Prentice-Hall of India Private Ltd., New Delhi
Prentice-Hall of Japan, Inc., Tokyo

Acknowledgments

Until recently, cat research lagged far behind that of other domestic animals. As a consequence, cat literature hasn't changed much over the past three decades. Now we know a great deal more about *Felis catus,* and the new information will be found on these pages. It came from many sources, and I wish to thank the following authorities, researchers, breeders and fanciers for their help:

Maxine Arps, Michael Brim, Jean Burden, James Corbin, Raymond Church VMD, Dorothea Cramer, Virginia Daly, Jean Ford, Vera Hill, Mrs. Jasperine Jones, Frances Kosierowski, Janet Mack, Jane Martinke, Evelyn Monte, Dorothy Murphy, May McAleenan, Kenneth McGill, R. P. Orman, and Patti O'Hern.

Also, Susie Page, Jean Rose, Mrs. Alex Ruzinski, Pam Sciacchitano, Leslie Smith, Raymond Smith, Mrs. Robert Treat, Katie Turner, Dr. Dean Casey White, Esther White, and Ethelyn Whittemore.

Also, officers of the various cat associations, American Museum of Natural History, American Veterinary Medical Association, Animal Welfare Institution, Carnation Company, *Cat Fancy, Cats Magazine,* Gaines Dog Research Center, Humane Society of the United States, Pet Pride, Inc., and Ralston Purina Company.

Also, the thousands of cats I've known and the many I've owned.

Kurt Unkelbach

Also by Kurt Unkelbach

RUFFIAN: INTERNATIONAL CHAMPION

MURPHY

THE DOG WHO NEVER KNEW

LOVE ON A LEASH

THE WINNING OF WESTMINSTER

THE DOG IN MY LIFE

BOTH ENDS OF THE LEASH:
SELECTING AND TRAINING YOUR DOG

A CAT AND HIS DOGS

contents

I.
any cat's story

Felis catus is his family name, and if numbers are considered proof of popularity, then he is the most popular pet animal on earth. And while he's unaware of the fact, he's the only pet who can claim two living ancestors from ancient times.

One is the wildcat, who still exists all over the world and is found in many parts of this country. He, of course, is the immediate ancestor of *Felis catus,* the *domestic* cat. And next in line behind the wildcat is the civet, who has been around for some ten million years and remains as a part of the wild animal population of Africa, Europe, Asia, China, India, and Malaya. In this country, civets are found only in zoos.

By studying the civet, scientists have been able to trace the history of the cat back to the original model, Miacis. He was a short-legged, long-bodied, ugly-headed, weasel-like creature who probably weighed no more than forty pounds and roamed the swamps and forests of the earth an estimated forty million years ago.

Strange as it may seem, the prehistoric Miacis was also the common ancestor of such familiar animals as the bear, the raccoon, the hyena, the weasel, and the dog. So the cat and the dog are related! They are very distant cousins, as distant as cousins can possibly be. Still, they are related, and that may be the reason why cats and dogs are not always the best of friends.

Just where and when the wildcat came to terms with man remains a mystery. A few experts point to India and China, but most agree that the pet cat came into being in the Egypt of five thousand years ago. Caffre, a wildcat still found along the Nile, closely resembles the pet cats we know today.

We do know that *Felis catus* was more abundant in ancient Egypt than in any other land. Five thousand years ago, Egypt was the grain capital of the world, but there was no convenient way to protect the granaries against the raiding armies of rats and mice until the cat came along. His excellent performance won the gratitude of a nation.

The thankful Egyptians brought him into their homes—hovels and palaces alike—and didn't treat him as an ordinary pet. For reasons beyond the understanding of modern man, they worshipped him. Laws were enacted to protect him; punishing him was a major crime, killing him or exporting him was a capital crime. He joined the baboon and the crocodile as a sacred animal. Pasht, the Egyptian goddess of life, had the body of a woman and the head of a cat.

It took a long time, but the ban on exporting did not stop foreign sailors from smuggling cats into the Southern Mediterranean countries of Europe. Over the centuries, domestic cats were introduced to all of Europe, and finally, thanks to the Roman Legions, to England. When the Romans sailed for home in the early years of the fifth century, they left *Felis catus* behind them.

Now the cat was known throughout the civilized world. The British didn't consider him a sacred animal, but the time came when they did enact laws to protect him. The first such law on record was dated 936 A.D., by order of the Prince of South Wales.

The cat's popularity continued to grow, until—during the Middle Ages—he became almost too popular for his own welfare. A Teutonic religious cult was spreading throughout Europe and threatening the power of the established Church. The cult had adopted and worshipped a Norse goddess named Freya, who rode around through the heavens in a chariot drawn by two giant, black cats.

The Church decided to fight Freya's followers by legalizing torture. Anyone suspected of worshipping Freya was arrested for sorcery and tortured, and ownership of a black cat was considered evidence of guilt. Women who owned black cats were considered to be witches, and men who owned black cats were devils in disguise. The humans weren't always tortured to death, but the cats always suffered that fate. Before long, ownership of any cat, black or non-black, was a sign of guilt.

That terrible time started late in the fifteenth century and lasted for over a hundred years. Hundreds of thousands of humans were killed, and so were millions of cats. Even after the senseless slaughter of humans ended, the cats were still fair game. Killing them was considered a sport. On religious festival days, hundreds at a time were burned to death as "an encouragement to morality." It's a wonder that any cats survived, but it should solve the riddle of why many people consider the black cat to be an unlucky sign.

There's no record of the first cat to reach America's shores. He wasn't on the Mayflower, nor was he here to greet the ship. The Indians had dogs, but not cats. However, we do know that some of the early settlers brought cats with them, and that, in colonial days when a woman was suspected of witchcraft, ownership of a cat didn't help her case.

It would seem that he achieved both pet and social status here at the same time. Some of the first Americans to acquire wealth imported cats from England. They paid high prices for their imports, but nothing like the prices paid by the new millionaires of the Gold Rush days. With money to burn and a desire to please their ladies, they thought nothing of paying two thousand dollars for a cat and then waiting six months for him to arrive from abroad.

The true American ascent of cat popularity started in 1895, the year of the first cat show on this side of the Atlantic. The original Madison Square Garden in New York City was the site. Fewer than two hundred cats were entered, but the event attracted thousands of spectators and was featured in major newspapers. The resultant publicity encouraged cat lovers in other areas to hold similar events, and within the space of a few years, major cities from coast to coast were hosts to cat shows. Fifteen to twenty thousand spectators were not unusual totals at those shows. Most people didn't understand what they were watching, but it didn't matter. They came to see the various breeds and colors of cats, and to order kittens from the breeders.

By the turn of the century, *Felis catus* had won his place as a beloved pet in the United States, but he still suffered from a rather strange sort of discrimination. Men continued to favor the dog over the cat.

Then came Slippers, a gray shorthair of unknown origins. He was just an ordinary cat, but he happened to be the favorite pet of President Theodore Roosevelt. Slippers became the first cat-in-residence at the White House. His presence there amounted to a vote of approval for all pet cats. Anti-cat sentiment started to fade.

There's no statue of Slippers in Washington, D.C., but cat lovers think there should be one. Some would be willing to settle for a Slippers postal stamp.

II.

the contemporary cat

He starts life as a *kitten,* of course, and at birth weighs about four ounces. His brothers and sisters, if he's going to have any, arrive at twenty to thirty minute intervals. One to four kittens comprise the average cat *litter,* although eight to ten is not unusual in some of the pure breeds, such as the Himalayan and Siamese.

His mother takes complete charge of him from the moment he's born. Except for her own meals, she needs no assistance from humans. She keeps him warm, dry, and clean, sees to it that he gets his share of her milk, and sleeps almost as much as he does.

For the first ten days, or until his eyes open, the new kitten nurses, sleeps, nurses, and sleeps again. He dines on the *queen's* milk—the only nourishment he needs—ten to twelve times a day, and sleeps the rest of the time.

Then, when vision comes, the kitten starts to become more active. He can already hear, taste, and smell, and now he sees—but not very much. All he sees is a blur, but it inspires him to move about,

inch about really, for he still lacks both strength
and coordination. If he goes anywhere in the next
couple of weeks, the queen will carry him there.

By his fourteenth day, the kitten sees distinctly,
but everything he sees is limited to tones of whites
and blacks and grays. It will always be that way for
him, for all cats are colorblind. None know it, of
course, and none suffer from it.

Day by day the kitten gains strength, and when
he's a month old he becomes a bit of a problem for
his mother. He's able to walk around on steady legs,

play with his litter mates, and do limited exploring on his own. And he requires more and more food.

The queen is able to provide him with enough milk, and is capable and willing to do so for at least another month, but now both his little teeth and claws are sharp. When she must nurse several kittens, feeding time starts to become hurting time for the queen.

With relief for her in mind, the wise owner starts *weaning* by offering a meal a day to the kitten. It's no trouble at all to teach a kitten that food is found in saucers as well as nipples, and some need no teaching.

Each week, the quantity of the food and the servings are increased. By the end of the eighth week, the kitten is completely weaned and no longer needs his mother's milk and care.

This is the ideal time for introducing the kitten to his new home.

The kitten grows in a hurry and is considered an adult at eight months. He's a cat now, and as big— or almost as big—as he'll ever be.

Man, not the cat, decided this age rule, and it is accepted throughout the world. The rule is mostly for the convenience of the cat show world, which has separate classes for kittens and cats. So a kitten is no longer a kitten when he's eight months old.

In a sense, the rule is a compromise between the sexes. The average male is not ready for breeding at eight months, but most females are ready at six and seven months of age, and some earlier than that. So the female develops much faster than the male, and many become mothers while they are still rated as kittens. That fact of cat life, plus irresponsible owners, is one of the major reasons why so many hundreds of thousands of unwanted kittens are born in this country every year.

No matter the breed, the average cat's life span is seventeen years. But it's not unusual for cats to live into their twenties, and rare ones achieve the thirties. The oldest cat on record was just over thirty-three.

Breed, inheritance factors, and health are all important in every cat's adult size. Males in the pink of condition average out between seven and ten pounds, and females run about a pound lighter. But fifteen-pounders aren't rare, and every so often a giant-sized twenty-five pounder comes along.

Almost always, overweight is caused by a wrong diet and lack of exercise, so it's not the cat's fault. Overeating is seldom the problem. From kittenhood on, he eats just enough to satisfy himself and no more. Still he's not food-wise in all respects, and doesn't really know what's bad for him. Every year, tens of thousands of kittens and cats die because they sampled poisons left within their reach by careless owners. All cats are inquisitive by nature, and that can lead to fatal trouble.

If he's a proper cat, his front paws boast five toes each and the rear ones have four. He always moves about on his toes, and no cat has ever been accused of being flatfooted. Each toe is host to a *retractable* claw, of course, and these claws are one of the cat's few imperfections. They come in handy for tearing things apart, fighting, and climbing trees, but they aren't designed for descending a tree head first. That's why kittens must be rescued from trees. Going up is no problem, but it takes a little experience to figure out how to come down. And the innocence of youth keeps him from jumping, although later he is an expert at judging distances and leaps only when sure that he'll safely reach his objective.

His tail runs from nothing at all (a good Manx) up to about eleven inches, and it comes in a variety of styles: stubby, long and thin, curled, and kinked. The experts have always regarded the cat's tail as his balancing agent, but that doesn't explain why the tailless Manx is as good on balance as any other cat. Other authorities argue that the tail is there as a means of communication, as sort of tail signals from one cat to another. There's no real way of proving or disproving that theory, but ardent cat lovers insist that the cat's tail communicates his mood. Thus, a swishing tail is a warning, a slowly waving tail denotes affection, an upright and curving tail spells contentment, and a ramrod stiff tail indicates concentration.

All those theories are fine, but all are full of loopholes. Now medical research has come up with a new theory: the tail is there to assist the cat's circulatory system. That doesn't explain the Manx, but he may be the exception to the rule. So there's confusion about the cat's tail, although everybody agrees that it adds to the cat's grace and beauty.

There's no confusion about those whiskers that are found up front. His whiskers and eyebrows provide him with the most delicate sense of touch in the whole animal kingdom. They are his guides in total darkness, and the foundation of the popular myth about cats being able to see in complete blackness. Every other hair on his body, tail included, is also sensitive to touch, and particularly those on his front paws.

His sense of hearing is also superior. High frequencies are his specialties, and often, when man thinks things are too quiet, the cat finds the world too noisy.

He has a most unusual and mysterious ear. Somehow, and nobody knows just how, the portion known as the inner ear gives the cat a unique balance and protects him against motion. Altitude won't make him dizzy, and he's never carsick or seasick. This helps explain why, when he falls a short distance, he usually lands on his feet.

And his is a very special eye. When hurt or ailing, a thin membrane known as a third eyelid closes over and protects the entire eyeball. In darkness, the pupil expands to soak in the ultra-violet rays man cannot distinguish; in bright light, the pupil closes to a mere slit and thus shuts out excess rays. The cat's shining eyes that peer out of the darkness at you are shining because iridescent cells on the retina are reflecting the available, dim light. So it's a special eye, and an odd one, too. Odd because the color of a kitten's eyes at the moment of birth are always blue. The color will darken, or change completely to another color, and many times one eye ends up a different color from the other.

While his eyes and ears are unusual, they are not as extraordinary as his brain. Although much smaller in size, it closely resembles the human brain—so closely that it has often been used by researchers studying our own thinking apparatus. While this doesn't mean that the cat has man's intelligence, *ailurophiles* regard the resemblance as evidence that the cat is smarter than any other animal.

It does increase his awareness and his ability to react, but it does not endow him with superior mental powers. While some cats are brighter than others, of course, the average cat rates a place or two behind the average dog in intelligence—or fourth or fifth place in the animal world, depending upon which authorities one cares to believe.

But no matter what research proves, there will always be room for debate. He's more difficult to train than a dog, but does this mean that he's stupid,

stubborn, or just too wise and independent to always please? And he will stare at something or somebody for long periods of time; does this mean that he's concentrating, or just waiting for a stray thought?

We're sure of one thing: he's more adaptable than a dog and better able to take complete care of himself. He can be a pet one day, and wander off into the unknown the next, live the life of a stray for weeks and months, then return home or settle down elsewhere and become the complete pet once again. Of the many millions of stray cats in America, some are strays by choice. It's a strange way to prove his intelligence, but perhaps all it proves is that there's a bit of gypsy in every cat.

III.

selecting the kitten

Sometimes he really selects you. You meet him on your doorstep, or along the road near your home, or on a path in the woods. And since you love animals, you want to keep the lonely, skinny kitten as a pet. There's no reason why you shouldn't. One of the finest cats the author's family ever owned was found in accidental fashion.

If you cannot keep him, the kind thing to do is to turn him over to the nearest humane society shelter. But if you do keep him, be sure that he receives more than simple nourishment. The probability is great that he has not received *preventive shots* against several dreaded, feline diseases, to which he may have already been exposed. A kitten's health is a delicate thing, and he's an easy victim for many illnesses that seldom bother an adult cat. So rush your new pet to the veterinarian as soon as possible.

There are other, simple ways to obtain a free kitten. In almost every neighborhood, somebody has free ones to give away. And it's a rare occasion for a daily or weekly newspaper when an edition doesn't carry at least one offer of free kittens to good homes. But in most cases, these gift kittens were unwanted in the first place. They were born because their *dams* were owned by careless, irresponsible people. It isn't likely that those owners spent an extra penny to guarantee the health of the kittens. So once again, if you accept a free kitten, rush him to the vet. A healthy pet makes the best pet.

Since there are always more kittens than willing homes, humane society shelters usually have an abundant supply on hand. They are the very best places to find your free kitten, for one of the main objectives of the societies is to find good homes for their pet animals, and they release only healthy individuals.

Still, it's always wise to question the health status of any kitten before taking him home. So look him over very carefully and check him on all of these points:

1) *Spirit:*   watch him in action. He should be aggressive, playful, and steady on his legs. If he stumbles about, he's too young to take home. There's a leader in every litter, and often he's the best bet. Always reject the timid, shy kitten who turns from you or hides in a corner.

2) *Coat:*   should be full, clean, and shiny. A dull, patchy coat means poor health. Bare spots are signs of skin infection.

3) *Mouth:*   a clear, rosy pink. Tongue always pink. A full set of clean white teeth in each jaw. If baby teeth are just breaking through gums, he's too young to leave his mother.

4) *Nose:*   moist and cool, never runny.

5) *Eyes:*   wide open, clear and bright, never squinty, watery or sticky. Wave something before his eyes to determine vision. If they blink, they see.

6) *Ears:*   clean, absolutely free of sores, scabs, and mites. Kittens with blue eyes and white kittens should always be tested for deafness. Test by making a noise (clap of hands, snap of fingers) behind head and watch for reaction.

7) *Body:* lean, but neither fat nor skinny. Stomach should be firm, never soft or bloated.

8) *Tail:* lift it and look for signs of diarrhea under vent and on backs of rear legs.

If the kitten of your choice passes all these tests, he's healthy—at that particular moment. Now for the double-check:

1) While examining the kitten, did you notice the smell of cat in the air? If so, there's something wrong somewhere. Offer a reasonable excuse to the owner and look elsewhere for your kitten.

2) If the air is clear, pick up that timid kitten and examine him. Chances are that he's not really shy, but just isn't feeling very well. If he can't pass the eight point program, then every other kitten present is a poor health risk. Offer your excuse, and better luck next time.

Now, if the double-check is all clear and you are buying the kitten, take advantage of every cat lover's private right and request a trial period of two or

three days. Explain that you consider the sale con-
ditional until your veterinarian gives the kitten a
good bill of health. If he doesn't, then you'll want to
return the kitten and recover your money. Any rep-
utable breeder will agree to such terms. Pet shops
often try to turn the agreement around and offer an
exchange of kittens. Don't fall for it. You may end up
with just another sick kitten.

Those free kittens are usually ones carrying short
coats. They come in many sizes, colors, and tail
lengths. They are popularly known as alley cats,
barn cats, and common cats, but in the *cat fancy*
they are respected as members of a definite breed:
the American Shorthair. In the dog fancy, a canine
of similar ancestry would be known as a cross breed
or a mongrel.

To avoid confusion, perhaps it would be best to
call the free kitten a plain American Shorthair, for
there is also a social American Shorthair. The latter
is more uniform in type, has a known pedigree, and
carries registration papers proving that he is a purebred. He and the kittens belonging to the other pure
breeds are seldom offered as gifts, unless one happens
to be a good friend of a breeder.

From a pet owner's point of view, there are certain
advantages in selecting a social or purebred kitten.
Thanks to the laws of inheritance, for example, it's
possible to predetermine the kitten's future in terms
of temperament, size, color, and—to a great degree
—intelligence.

The purebred's registration papers are important
for anyone interested in becoming a breeder and

making a little money on the side. And for anyone interested in entering his pet in cat shows, only the purebreds are eligible to compete for the titles of Champion, Grand Champion, and International Champion.*

Pet shops, private breeders, and *catteries* are the sources of the purebreds, and prices cover a wide range. In general, pet shops offer the lowest prices, and also the greatest risk. Unless the owner of the shop happens to be a breeder, or is known to have excellent breeder contacts, that source is the poorest bet.

The private breeders and catteries are the safest sources, for their reputations are on the line and their prices must be competitive. And importantly, they don't stay in business unless they sell healthy kittens. Most provide a veterinarian's certificate of good health, and all the best ones do. Further, they offer sound advice on feeding and care.

Unlike the market in purebred puppies, each kitten in a given litter often carries a different price tag. The best specimens, or those who seem to have the strongest potential for showing or breeding or both, bring the top dollars. But there are usually at least a couple of kittens in every purebred litter who do not have that potential; perhaps their colors are a bit light, or their heads a touch too round. These kittens have all the virtues of their litter mates, make

---

* By winning two championships—one in the U.S.A. and the other in Canada—a cat becomes an International Champion.

fine pets, sell for much less, and only an expert knows that they lack show promise. Thus the price range for a given litter may run from twenty dollars up to a hundred and fifty dollars and more. And often the twenty-dollar kitten will fool the experts and mature into a better show cat than his expensive brother.

Cat lovers are evenly divided over the question of sex. Does the male kitten make a better pet than the female? All other qualities (health, temperament, and intelligence) being equal, the question of sex is unimportant in kittenhood. The problems begin when the kitten reaches maturity. The male *sprays* everything in sight, and the spray carries a strong, unpleasant odor. He also spends a great deal of time away from home, engaged in romance and cat fights. During her breeding seasons (usually twice a year), the female will also stray from home to find a mate. If confined, she will sing her yearnings at any hour of the day and night. Her *callings* are sort of a cross between a wail and a screech, and all tomcats within a range of several miles will arrive in the yard and engage in fights while waiting for her to appear.

Fortunately, it's easy to avoid all of those problems, if all you want is a pet and companion. The avoidance is something called *neutering,* and it means *altering* the male or *spaying* the female. There's nothing dangerous about this operation, although it should always be handled by a vet. As a result, the kittens grow into cats who can never become parents.

From twelve to sixteen weeks of age is the time to neuter a kitten. The operation can be performed at any age, but the younger the better. Neutered males don't *spray,* stray, or go around looking for fights. Neutered females don't call, stray, or present you with unwanted kittens. And usually the neutered pet's longevity is increased.

No matter how one looks at it, neutering makes great sense. If our country's pet owners would make use of that common sense, we wouldn't have millions of unwanted kittens, and millions of stray cats, and perhaps there'd be a loving home for every cat.

IV.

cats in america

The United States of America leads the world in such areas as gross national income, average personal income, steel production, communications, and total number of cats. While it would be impossible to arrive at an exact total, the findings of many interested groups (humane societies, federal and state agencies, universities, and the pet food industry) place our feline population at about the fifty million mark.

Even that grand total may be low, for it includes ten million *feral,* or wild, cats, and there may be fifteen million of them. But if we accept the ten million figure, we can still claim forty million non-feral or pet cats.*

And that's another deceptive total. Nobody knows how many millions of those forty are sort of half-pet cats, or the ones who have no real homes or

* But if every kitten born managed to survive, we would soon have more cats than people. Because sufficient proper homes can't be found and some of their wards are beyond saving, humane societies in New York City alone must destroy over a hundred thousand kittens and cats every year.

owners. They live in barns, sheds, garages, and under porches, accepting hand-outs from people, and moving along to new locations when the regular hand-outs disappear. They are constantly looking for permanent homes and usually never find them.

Thirty million pet cats would be a reasonable total, a figure that would still give us first place in the world over such other cat-loving countries as England, Italy, Belgium, Denmark, Norway, Sweden, Austria, and Switzerland. There's a plentitude of cat lovers and cats in almost every country, including Russia, where the common cat is the Russian Blue. *Cats Magazine,* the only literature read by many ardent cat fanciers, has subscribers in such countries as India, Saudi Arabia, Thailand, Guatemala, Martinique, Australia, Japan, and Monaco.

About eighty pure breeds of cats exist in the world. There will never be fewer, for every so often man, thanks to his knowledge of *selective breeding,* develops a new breed from two or more of the existing ones.

Representatives of thirty-six of the pure breeds are known to be in the United States. Of these, only twenty-three are recognized by one or more of the governing bodies in America that control the registrations of cats, approve breed *standards,* and set the rules and regulations for the cat shows. Cats of these breeds, registered or eligible for registration, are the elite, or the superior members, of our cat population. They also represent a minority group. Of the thirty million pet cats, only two million are purebreds, but no more than three hundred thousand of them are registered.

The records show that only thirty thousand* of the elite were registered last year, but this figure is expected to double within the next five years. There are abundant signs to prove that the whole cat fancy is booming: sales of manufactured cat foods are zooming, breeders are on the increase, pet stores sell more kittens than pups, prices for some purebreds now rival those asked for purebred pups, there are more cat shows every year, and the list of local cat clubs keeps growing.

Now, just in case you're interested in purchasing an elite kitten, let's look at the pure breeds recognized on our side of the Atlantic.

* For comparison, American Kennel Club registrations are close to one million a year. This doesn't mean that there are more dogs than cats in this country, but that there are many more purebred dogs than purebred cats.

Only six of the pure breeds are longhairs. They are considered the beauties of the cat world, but forget them if you can't find a little time each day to comb and brush their coats. All do their best to groom themselves, but these long hairs pick up so many things—dirt, burrs, bits of leaves and grass—and will matt in a hurry. They require less coat care if kept indoors, of course, and are more popular in the city than the country. But when he sheds, the indoor longhair can be a nuisance for perfectionist housekeepers.

PERSIAN

PERSIAN

The uninformed call him the Angora, but that breed hasn't been around for some years. In numbers, the Persian is the king of the longhairs, and his admirers insist that he's the quietest and most affectionate of all the breeds. His coat comes in a variety of more than twenty colors, and under the coat is a deep chest and chunky body. He is one of the oldest pure breeds known to man. There's a lesser known variety of this breed known as the Peke-Face. The head resembles that of the Pekingese dog, the coat color is always red, and the eyes are copper. He is ideal for anyone who wants an odd-looking cat.

HIMALAYAN

Californians should be proud of this new longhair breed, for it was developed there after World

HIMALAYAN

War II. Just imagine the Persian with the coat colors (light body, dark *points*) plus red of the shorthair Siamese, and you have the Himalayan. Nothing strange about that, for the two breeds were successfully crossed to produce the newcomer, who is rapidly gaining in poularity.

BALINESE

Another new breed. This fellow looks like a Siamese in a fur coat, and that's what he really is: a longhair version of the Siamese. Under the two-inch or more coat is the long, sleek body of his cousin, and that's how to distinguish him from a Himalayan of identical color.

Only one breed, the Rex, sports a wavy coat, and thus becomes sort of a compromise between the longhairs and the shorthairs. An excellent choice for anyone who wants something unusual in cats.

REX

Tight waves of silky, dense coat extend from the top of the head and across the back to the tip of the tail, and down sides and hips. The coat comes in many colors. Long legs, an arched back, and power-ful quarters put him in a class by himself, for no other breed matches his speed or his high jumping. If you ride a horse and would like cat company on the trails, you won't outdistance this fellow.

The Rex and the other recognized breeds except for three are classified as shorthairs, and for the very best reasons: short hair is dominant over long hair. It's possible for mated shorthairs to produce a longhair kitten, but impossible for mated long-hairs to produce a shorthair kitten. It's a matter of genes.

The short coat, of course, makes grooming a simple matter for the owner. A couple of grooming sessions a week will keep coat and skin in prime condition. The shorthair can almost take care of himself.

REX

SIAMESE

SIAMESE

Easily the most popular of the pure breeds, he outnumbers all of the longhair breeds combined. He chatters more than any other breed, so forget him if you're looking for a quiet cat. Many people find his personality somewhat doglike, and it's a fact that centuries ago he was employed as a watch-cat at temples in Siam. Oddly, he stands much higher in the rear than the front, but this seems to help the graceful movements of his long and slender body. He comes in chocolate, seal, blue, and lilac (frost) *point* colors. The body is always a lighter shade of the points.

ABYSSINIAN

Despite rumors to the contrary, this breed was developed in England about a century ago. One of the smallest breeds, intelligent, a home lover, and easy to train, he should be much more popular than he is. Unfortunately, he's difficult to breed, litters are small, and most kittens are males. He's hard to locate, and females cost more than males. The coat comes in two shades of brown (ruddy and red), plus brown and black *tickings*. His body is slim, medium long, fine boned and well balanced. Obviously, this isn't a breed for ambitious breeders.

ABYSSINIAN

AMERICAN SHORTHAIR

AMERICAN SHORTHAIR

Also known as Domestic Shorthair, this is now believed to be the original domestic cat, and among the purebreds he's second in rank to the Siamese. Many authorities rate him as the best all-around cat, for he's quite self sufficient. A fine house pet and a noted stalker of rodents, he adapts easily to any new situation, and—when lost—can get along very well on his own. His coat comes in solid, mixed, and *tabby* colors. The asking price is usually modest.

BURMESE

Another of the doglike breeds, the Burmese is gentle, friendly, quiet, and easy to train on a collar and leash. Despite the name, the breed didn't come from Burma and may have been developed in the United States. In maturity, his coat is a rich, chocolate brown, and his big, round eyes range from

BURMESE

yellow to brilliant gold. A green-eyed Burmese is not considered proper. One of the most beautiful of the shorthairs, this breed is moving ahead in popularity.

HAVANA BROWN

In this breed, only green eyes are proper, and the right coat color is a mahogany (tobacco) brown. This is another man-made breed, and so new that it's only been known in this country for about a dozen years. The Havana originated in England (where he's known as the Chestnut Brown), and the Siamese is one of the breeds behind him. However, the Havana has oval-shaped rather than Oriental eyes, a shorter tail, a more compact body, and a quieter personality. There are not many around as yet, but breeders have no trouble selling their kittens.

RED COLORPOINT

Well, you must understand the cat fancy to understand why this is a separate breed. He's the Siamese all over again, except that he carries colors not recognized by the Siamese set. His points are a deep red, and his body coat is white, or white with light shadings of the red. This is also the fifth color combination of the Himalayan. It's difficult to achieve the red color, so maybe the Red Colorpoint deserves to be a separate breed. Another name for him is the Shorthair Colorpoint.

MANX

This is the famous (and only) tailless breed. A good one has a hollow at the end of his spine, where a tail would normally sit. Lack of tail plus

MANX

shorter front legs than rear give him a stilted walk and a rabbit-like fast gait. Of solid compact build, he's a great hunter of rodents and usually loves swimming. But he's not much of a climber and thus hardly a menace to songbirds. He's not any easy breeder: any litter can produce a few imperfect kittens with stump tails or short tails. Of all the cat breeds, dogs respect the Manx. The tailless one loves to guard his home grounds. He comes in a wide choice of coat colors.

RUSSIAN BLUE

Cat fanciers have been arguing over the origin of this breed for a long time, so we'll never know if he's Russian or not. But he did come here from Europe, via England. The light blue coat and green eyes make him one of the more beautiful shorthairs, but beauty isn't everything, and he's not as popular today as he was thirty years ago. Fine bones, small paws, slender body, and tapering tail help his grace of movement. He's a quiet breed and a lover of solitude.

Those twelve pure breeds are recognized by all eight of America's cat governing bodies.* There are more pure breeds, but none are currently recognized by all the governing bodies. It takes a long time to achieve unanimous recognition. While they await that glorious day, these breeds remain unaware of the situation and consider themselves the social equals of the other twelve.

* See Glossary for names and addresses

BRITISH BLUE

A husky version of the Russian Blue, he also has a different eye color: orange, varying from yellow to copper. He's the pride and joy of England, but he's never really caught on with the cat fancy here. Black kittens often pop up in a litter, for blue is really a *sport* of black. The Britisher is a calm fellow, and thus ideal for indoor living. But there aren't many around, so kittens command high prices.

KORAT

Introduced to this country from Thailand within the past decade, this breed is gaining in popularity and prices are leveling off. His big green eyes, curved back line, and silver-sheened blue coat set him apart from other breeds. His many admirers claim that he's quiet, friendly, playful, and anxious to please.

EXOTIC SHORTHAIR

A big, round head, a snub nose, short legs, and a tail that always slants downwards distinguish this fellow from the American Shorthair. Like the American, his coat comes in over twenty solid color and color combinations. And he has the same self-confidence, which means that he likes to see the world. Neutering will help to keep him at home.

MAINE COON CAT

This is the fourth of the longhair breeds, and one of the biggest of all the breeds. His pointed ears seem oversized, and his tail is exceptionally long. Husky in build, he comes in a variety of colors and is famous as a rat chaser, tree climber, swimmer, and also as the one cat who doesn't mind extreme cold. There's Persian behind him, but otherwise his bloodlines are unknown. As Maine goes, so goes the nation, and he's been a favorite in Maine for a long time. Farmers there insist that the Maine Coon is a cross between a cat and a raccoon, although it's impossible for cats and raccoons to interbreed. Still, it's a good story, and this is a fine cat. A great choice if you insist on a longhair breed, for his coat runs a bit shorter than those of the other longhairs.

SACRED CAT OF BURMA

Here we go again: a breed with the same color points as the Siamese. However, this fellow carries white *gloves* on all four paws. White almost covers the front paws and does cover the rear ones, and also *laces* up the hock to a point. Of all the longhairs, his coat is the silkiest, seldom matts, and that makes him the easiest of the longhairs to groom. A French breed, he's unknown in Burma, but is a forty-year resident in the United States. So few are around that most cat fanciers have never seen one.

OCICAT

New and not widely known as yet, this big, rangy hybrid (Siamese and Abyssinian) has a satiny, cream coat that carries chestnut spots. His eyes are always golden, his nose and paw pads pink. Long in legs, body and tail, he moves with the grace of an ocelot, but fortunately he's not related. He is priced high and worth the money.

LONGHAIR MANX

When you see a longhaired cat without a tail, you're looking at a Longhair Manx. He's the sixth and the last of the longhairs, and a hybrid (Manx and Persian). The coat comes in only six different colors, compared to his Manx (Shorthair) ancestor's twenty-one.

MANXAMESE

A Manx carrying any one of the four color points of the Siamese is not a Manx. He's a Manx-amese and a *hybrid* (Manx and Siamese) and another new arrival on the scene. Those colors guarantee his popularity, and prices are coming down.

COLORPOINT

Refer to the Red Colorpoint. This is the same cat, but he carries eight more point colors, including all those of the Siamese, and that makes him a separate breed. That's how the cat fancy goes.

LAVENDER FOREIGN SHORTHAIR

This hybrid (Siamese and Havana Brown) is one of the gentlest breeds around. A male will often try to take care of kittens. Similar in build to the Siamese, but heavier in bone, the Lavender's coat is a solid *mauve* shade. A good one has big ears, a wedged head, and deep green eyes that are almond-shaped. Most breeders are in Southern California. He is difficult to breed, and never found at bargain prices.

HARLEQUIN

Once known as the Ming (he dates back to 15th–century China), this is the only spotted white cat. A good one carries a single black spot on his head, none or up to ten on his body, and a solid black, blunt tail. The dense coat covers a Manx-like body, and its spots are the size of fifty-cent pieces. This quiet, gentle fellow is a great favorite in Japan, where he is regarded as a fine pet. Although the first ones reached this country in 1900, Harlequin kittens are still hard to find and bring top prices.

Those are the twenty-three pure breeds recognized in the United States and Canda. If you can't find the breed that strikes your fancy through normal channels (advertisements, breeders, veterinarians), visit a cat show. There you'll find out who has kittens for sale.

Be forewarned that your first visit to a cat show may not be your last one. Cat show fever may infect you, and you'll want to win a championship for your pet.

Cat shows are much more democratic than dog shows, where only purebreds who are *whole* may compete for a title. While only a whole, purebred cat can win the title of champion, there are other titles for neutered, purebred cats, and honors for common cats in the Household Pet division. So even

non-purebred cats are welcome at cat shows. There's
no age limit for owners, but kittens must be at least
four months old.

The governing bodies work with the local member
cat clubs that hold the licensed cat shows. These
are the shows where titles are won, and about two
hundred and fifty of them are held in this country
every year. So long as the kitten or cat is healthy,
well-groomed, clean, and friendly enough to be

handled by strangers (show judges), he's welcome. No special training is required, but it's always a good idea to accustom the pet to show excitement by entering him first in informal shows. While official titles can't be won at these shows, they are fine training grounds. About a thousand of them are held from coast to coast every year, and they are announced under a variety of names: Kitten Show, Novice Cat Show, Household Pet Show, and Kitten or Cat Match Show.

It takes a good cat to become a Champion, and a great one to become a Grand Champion. And every year, the greatest of the great becomes Cat Of The Year.* In a sense, this annual award is the only constant thing about the cat show world, for the eight governing bodies vary as to their rules, regulations, breed standards, and procedures. For over half a century, reasonable cat fanciers have been trying to achieve uniformity among the governing bodies. While each body would retain its own identity, all would abide by the rules, regulations, and standards set by the International Cat Associations. This goal will become a reality someday, and then the ICA will simplify things for everybody concerned: the general public, the cat fancy, and the cats.

But that day isn't here yet. Proving, perhaps, that cat fanciers disagree just as much as a *clowder* of cats.

---

* *Cats Magazine* keeps the records and makes the award. The winner defeats about ten thousand other cats at shows during the year.

There are a sufficient number of breeds around to satisfy the most discriminating of cat lovers. One might not think so, however, after talking to certain animal dealers and cat owners who insist that only the *exotic* cats—the wild cousins of the domestic cat —make the very best pets. Tens of thousands of people who want to own a different sort of pet cat now share their homes with pet ocelots, margays, cheetahs, and jaguarandis. All these animals are sold when they are kittens and command high prices.

The urge to own something different is understandable. But despite glowing accounts in the magazines and the press about the desirability of exotic cats as pets, all spell trouble, and you would be wise to forget them. Cute and tame as they are as kittens, all do grow, and once they reach adulthood none can be trusted. Then they become dangerous. Not dangerous to the furniture, necessarily, but dangerous to you and your family and friends.

To keep them in the best of health, they require expensive, special diets. Most veterinarians are not qualified to treat them, and those that are would rather not touch them. In many communities, local laws forbid ownership. And it's difficult, often impossible, to find a new home for one. Zoos have an ample supply of better specimens, humane shelters won't accept them, and you can't give them to friends. In addition, the cats can carry diseases that you might catch from them.

And if all those facts don't deter you, consider this one: in the unnatural environment and conditions of domestic life, exotic cats seldom live more than three or four years. So owners are due for early heartaches.

Still unconvinced? Then consider this sad fact of life: there aren't any breeders of exotic cats. Thus the kittens offered for sale had to be captured when very young. And how does a hunter capture an exotic kitten? By shooting his mother, of course.

If you have ever owned a pet monkey, then you have some slight idea of the trouble people have in raising a pet from the wild. So be wise, be happy, be satisfied: stay with *Felis catus*.

If you can afford to buy a purebred kitten, do so. He's your best guarantee of overall health and quality, especially if you buy directly from his breeder.

While all of the pure breeds make ideal pets (just ask their breeders), some require more time and care than others. That's true of all the longhairs.

The best three breeds for young cat lovers are all shorthairs: American Shorthair, Burmese, and Rex. All are quiet, intelligent, easy to train, adaptable and responsive, and require minimum care. Only the American comes in a big variety of colors and color combinations.

Kitten prices vary around the country, but almost anywhere it's possible to find a pet quality American for fifteen or twenty dollars, and a Burmese or Rex for ten or fifteen dollars more. On the other hand, since most breeders love cats and consider breeding a hobby and not a business, a token payment of five or ten dollars will often buy a kitten. Many breeders are more interested in finding good homes for their kittens than they are in profit.

If you are not interested in showing or breeding, you'll save yourself a lot of headaches by neuturing your cat. Every vet has his own price for this safe operation, and most charge from ten to twelve dollars. The all important *preventive shots* will run from seven to ten dollars.

As for upkeep, it costs more to feed a kitten than a cat. If you must buy all of the kitten's food, the monthly cost will be around five dollars. Food for the adult cat will run from nothing to three dollars, depending on your ability to borrow from the refrigerator and save table scraps. Unfortunately, the free kitten costs as much to feed as the purchased kitten.

kitten care and training

With your help, the kitten is ready to start his pet career when he's eight weeks old. If you have any say in the matter, eight to ten weeks is the ideal time to bring him home. He's ready to adjust to a new situation and his brain power is beginning to function.

If you've purchased him, you have every right to insist that he's already received at least temporary immunization against two diseases: feline enteritis and pneumonitis. Both diseases are dangerous and highly contagious, and any healthy kitten can pick them up. Then the kitten doesn't have much chance. Hardly any, in the case of enteritis, and less than fifty percent with pneumonitis. People who claim those immunizations are useless and silly are among the uninformed. Kittens by the thousands don't last through the first week in their new homes, but those are the ones nobody talks about.

The odds are a thousand to one against the free kitten having any shots. By all means, use your head and rush him to the vet.

Now let's look at some of the necessary preparations for the newcomer in your life:

Bed

A cardboard carton is great for a starter. Cut an entrance hole in one end, line with folded newspaper, a piece of old blanket, or soft rags. Place the bed away from human traffic and keep it free of drafts and bright lights. The kitten will fall asleep everywhere else the first few days. When he does, pick him up and place him in his own bed. He'll soon know it's his.

Sanitary Pan

When nature calls, it should call him to a definite place. Half fill a shallow metal pan with shredded paper, sawdust, or one of the commercial cat litter products. Do not change location of the pan. Place him in the pan whenever he awakens, after playtimes, and after every meal. Most kittens learn where to go in the first day. Occasional accidents may happen for a couple of weeks, but usually you'll find that somebody closed a door and the kitten couldn't get to his pan.

Clean the pan and replace litter at least twice daily, or more often should the aroma dictate.

For pan litter, the author uses sawdust or wood shavings and places the pan on the far end of a good sized, newspaper-lined cardboard box. The entrance hole is cut in near end. The sides of the box keep litter from scattering about room. Neat kittens love to dig and bury, and sawdust does fly.

Understanding

This means not the kitten's sense of understanding, but yours. Despite his activity and wise-looking eyes, he's a baby, knows next to nothing, and can't take care of himself. It's up to you to keep him safe. Indoors, that means keeping him away from open windows, placing poisons out of his reach, and making sure the screen is in front of the fireplace. Outdoors, it means keeping him off the street, away from open wells, and free from the society of bees, porcupines, skunks, and adult pet animals. Always keep an eye on him. He'll want to roam, and he can get lost fifty feet from your back door.

Try to appreciate his new world through his eyes. It's full of two-legged giants, strange noises and scents, and lifeless things that move around on wheels. It all adds up to a frightening experience for the baby. Help him to settle down by giving him plenty of love and companionship. Play with him, and let him get used to his name. But don't tire him, and wait a couple of weeks before you introduce him to all your friends. There's plenty of time.

From eight weeks to nine months, the kitten passes through the period of his greatest growth. He eats more per day than he ever will as an adult, and always—from his first day to his last—he doesn't seem to know what's bad for him.

Like the brain, the cat's digestive system is constructed along lines similar to man's. However, there's a big difference: the cat's digestive tract has difficulty handling starchy foods, probably because he doesn't need them. So go easy on any portions of potato, corn, baked goods, macaroni and the like.

The most important nutrient in his diet is protein. It should amount to forty percent of his daily intake, since his body functions just can't get along without it. He requires fats, vitamins, minerals, and water, too, if you want him to say healthy and happy, and keep his coat shiny.

Right now, let's look at a good, daily menu for the growing kitten:

Eight to Twelve Weeks of Age

Feed four times a day: about two ounces of baby meat, finely ground meat or kidney, or cooked or canned fish in tiny pieces; add yolk of one raw egg, once a day; add sufficient whole milk to create a sort of thick soup.

Be careful about two things: (1) always remove bones, and (2) never serve cold meals—warm or room temperature is best.

As for milk, don't believe everything you've heard. A kitten needs a couple of cups daily, but an adult cat often turns up his nose at the white stuff. But at any age, his body requires lots of liquid, so keep a pan of fresh water (never cold) handy for him at all times.

Give the kitten plenty of time to finish his meal, but pick up his meal when he seems satisfied. Some will eat a little less than the amount given above, and some will need more. Don't worry about overeating, for he seems to know his own capacity.

Twelve to Twenty Weeks of Age

Feed three times a day: stay with the same basic
    diet, but increase meat or fish portions to satisfy
    growing appetite; add a handful of *kibble* to at
    least one meal; add a couple of tablespoons of
    a baby vegetable to another; and an ounce of
    fine liver or heart to the third.

Check him every couple of days to make sure that
he's in lean condition, but not thin. He's too thin if
any rib bones are protruding.

Twenty to Thirty-two Weeks of Age

Fccd two times a day: raw or cooked (especially
    pork) meats, heart, beef livers, kidneys, cooked
    poultry, cooked or canned (mackerel is dandy)
    fish should total about four ounces per meal;
    bulk should be kibble, vegetables, and milk, and
    egg yolk can be cut down to one every couple
    of days.

By now the kitten's baby teeth are gone and he
has his full set of permanent grinders. This means
that his meat, fish or fowl can bc served in small
pieces, and cut up raw vetetables can be substituted

for the cooked ones. Remember about the starches, however, and go easy on potato, corn, and the like.

For the transition from three to two meals a day, the author takes about ten days, and does this by gradually reducing the size of the mid-day meal.

At the end of thirty-two weeks, the kitten becomes a cat. He should remain on two meals a day until he's one year old, but gradually increase the morning meal and decrease the evening one. After one year, any cat should be able to get by on one big meal a day, but some think they have been robbed and create so much noise that only a second meal will quiet them. In such cases, make the big meal the morning one and give him just a snack in the evening.

Adults vary as to their food requirements, and the average cat will need from four to seven ounces of meat (or fish or poultry) per day, or enough to satisfy his protein needs. He must have fat, too, and that's the other reason for meats, as well as egg yolks and liver. The meats, kibble, and vegetables also give him sufficient vitamins and minerals. Some people insist on adding commercial pet vitamins to his food. They do no harm.

Of course, he always needs plenty of water, for it amounts to about three-quarters of his body weight and helps lubricate his various organs. He must have it available. Even if he drinks a gallon of milk a day, he still needs fresh water.

The easiest way to feed a kitten or a cat, is, of course, to stock up on a supply of the canned and packaged commercial cat foods available at pet shops and supermarkets. While they may not be money savers, they are time savers, and several excellent brands have appeared on the market in recent years. Should you favor this method of feeding, be sure to check the labels and make certain that the food contains close to forty percent protein and twenty-five percent fat.

Now for that orphan kitten—or the one you find on your doorstep some sunny morning. Chances are that he'll be younger than eight weeks, and a kitten's size is not an indicator of his age. Use his teeth to estimate his age:

> If fewer than twenty-six baby teeth are showing, he's four to five weeks old.
>
> If all his twenty-six baby teeth are showing, he's at least five weeks old.
>
> If the teeth are well formed and sharp, he's six to seven weeks old.

At those tender ages, their tiny stomachs are no bigger than a walnut, and they can't stow away much food at one sitting. So they must dine five or six times a day, and whole milk satisfies their needs at four to five weeks. Always serve it as close to the cat's normal body temperature (101.5°) as possible. A drop on your wrist that feels mildly warm is close enough. Serve in a shallow saucer. This may puzzle him, for his only food source may have been his mother's nipple. So wet your finger in the milk a few times, and let him lick off the milk. Then daub a little milk on his nose. He'll learn to lap from the saucer in a hurry.

At five weeks, stay with the milk, but add a tablespoon of pablum twice a day.

At six weeks, continue with milk and pablum, but add yoke af raw egg once a day.

At seven weeks, continue with milk, pablum, and egg yolk, but add two tablespoons of baby meat to at least two meals.

Usually, kittens are not fussy eaters, but many adult cats are. When your pet turns up his nose at some perfectly good food, remove it and re-offer at the next regular meal time. If he continues to reject the food, either he's not feeling well or is acting plain stubborn.

If there's anything wrong with him, his temperature will be more than one degree (higher or lower) off normal. Also, he'll probably want to be alone and will hide in some dark, sheltered place.

If he appears to be in good health, then he's probably acting stubborn and wants another food that he prefers. Now the choice is yours. Do you want a pampered pet? One thing always leads to another, and the more you spoil him, the more he'll want to be spoiled.

It's best to keep offering him the same food over and over again at meal times until—finally—he starts to eat again. You can be sure that he will, just as soon as he's hungry enough. A healthy cat can go several days without solid food, before he gives in.

There's nothing cruel about this method and it amounts to common sense. After all, the cat is your pet. You are not his.

Although he'll soon understand a few words through association—his name and some commands, for example—even the kitten who is anxious to please won't understand what you are saying. He relies solely on his instincts for his actions. Handle him roughly and he'll defend himself with teeth and claws. Shout at him or throw things at him and he'll run away.

Today's kitten is tomorrow's cat, and the molding of his personality is in your hands. With a little thought, you can teach him to be a joy and not a nuisance, a perfect pet rather than a household pest. Here are some training hints:

Naming the Kitten

A short name is better than a long one. Fritz is better than Clarence. Easier for you to say and easier for him to recognize. From the very beginning, use his name frequently, whether you think what you're saying to him makes sense or not. Thus: "Fritz, you're a good kitten" when you're petting him, or "Fritz, come," when you serve his meals, or "Fritz, no!" when you remove him from the table.

Try to use his name first whenever you address him. Within a week, he'll know the name is his.

Handling the Kitten

Never pick him up by the scruff of the neck or by his tail. True, his mother may have carried him by the scruff of the neck, but he was helpless then and you're not his mother. Now he has teeth and claws.

So put one hand under his chest, using your fingers to hold his forelegs. Place the other hand under his buttock. Now lift him.

Scratching

Instinct tells the kitten to keep his claws (nails) sharp and down to a length that won't impede his walking. So he needs something to scratch, and almost anything will do: a table leg, a rug, a drape, or stuffed furniture.

To prevent such activity, many owners provide scratching posts. These may be purchased at any pet shop, or you can make one yourself. Select a log about twenty inches long and four to five inches in diameter. Cover with a couple of thicknesses of old rug or carpet. Secure this covered log in vertical position to a solid base—so solid that the log won't topple. If the kitten doesn't prefer this to a table leg, then rub some catnip on the covering.

This works with the average kitten, but yours may not be average. If that's the case, the best thing to do is to keep his nails a proper length by trimming them. Inexpensive nail clippers can be purchased at any pet shop. Press lightly on the kitten's paw and his nails will shoot out into the open. Cut back the transparent portion just short of the quick (vein). Check nails every few weeks.

Start trimming his nails when he's a kitten and he won't resent the action when he becomes a cat. It will cut down on his songbird hunting, too.

Then, for the rare cat who insists on clawing and destroying, there's always declawing. This calls for a surgical operation. The nails are removed and never grow in again. Declawing is used as a last resort by owners who want to keep their otherwise incurable cats. It's fine for the cat who spends all his time indoors, but places the part-time outdoor cat at an obvious disadvantage. Declawing also disqualifies a cat for showing.

Idle Hours

Boredom is a fact of animal life, too, and it's the bored kitten who goes looking for trouble. Since you won't be supervising your pet every minute of the day and night, provide him with a few playthings. Pet shops are full of toys for him, but there's no reason to invest in anything if you use your imagination. Hard rubber balls, big knuckle bones, empty spools of thread, twisted lengths of paper, paper bags, open cardboard containers, lengths of string tied to a doorknob all make fine kitten toys and help fill his idle hours.

Just be sure that anything he demolishes and eats can't harm him.

VI.

the obedient cat

The cat has always been noted for his spirit of independence. In the wild, he prefers to live alone. When several pet cats are under one roof, each prefers to go his own way and they seldom engage in group activity.

This independence is often mistaken for intelligence. "The cat is too smart, and you can't teach him to do anything he doesn't want to do," is a popular belief of our times. "He's too smart for people" is another version of the same theory, and one of the reasons why there are so many spoiled, untrained pet cats in the world.

His intelligence doesn't amount to much in comparison to that of a human. Your's is vastly superior, even if it did take you three years to graduate from the first grade.

But the cat is intelligent enough to enjoy having his own way so long as people insist on giving it to him. He would be an absolute fool if he reacted otherwise. He appreciates easy living just like anyone else. He is given food, protection, shelter, and love, and very little is asked of him in return. Who could ask for anything more?

The fact is that a pet cat can be trained, and the whole truth is that it takes double patience to train him. Normal patience, as in the case of training the dog, isn't enough. True, the kitten is easier to house-break than the pup, but that's a matter of instinct, not brain power. The cat is naturally neat. His many talents are all based on instincts. Otherwise, he's a slow learner. Not because he's brilliant and insists on his independence, but because he's not brilliant and it takes him a long time to learn something new.

The easiest (but not recommended) way to train him is through the use of fear. Put his dinner dish down in a new place and notice how he looks in all directions and doesn't dine until he's sure that he's safe. And watch him when he hears a strange noise. He's alert and ready to run from danger.

His still-wild relatives—the lions and tigers and leopards—are all familiar performers at the circus and in films. All are trained through fear to do their tricks. The snapping whip that sends the lion flying through the hoop is a reminder of punishment he's endured behind the scenes in training.

Of course, no person in his right mind wants to train his pet cat that way, for it amounts to cruelty.

The only other way to achieve sure results is to employ double patience. But don't start the training too early, or you won't get any results, and even your triple patience will wear thin. Four months is young enough to start teaching him a few things, but teach him one thing at a time.

Here are some practical things for him to learn:

Coming When Called

At meal time, rap the dish as you put it down and call out "Fritz, come!" Don't be overjoyed when he comes, for he'll come as soon as he spots the dish anyway. Still, after several days of hearing the word "come," he'll start associating it with pleasure.

Then use the same words in calling him to you from across the room. When he responds, by design or accident, play with him or offer him a tidbit (a bit of mild cheese, liver, fish, or a commercial pet treat). Something pleasant should happen when he comes. Once he does come, don't overdo it, and don't call him when you don't have time for him.

This is a good test of your double patience. You may have to test it for two or three weeks.

Curing the Beggar

A lively kitten will climb into your lap and from there scramble onto the table whenever you sit down to your own meals. Whenever he does this, (1) tap his paws, but not severely, (2) say "Fritz, no!" in a firm tone of voice and (3) pick him up and place him on the floor. If he grasps the idea within two days, you have a pet with above average intelligence.

Of course, you can keep him on the floor by offering tidbits from your own plate, but that's just teaching him to be a nuisance.

Or you can avoid the whole problem by arranging his meals to coincide with your own.

Off Limits

In many households, pets are not permitted on the furniture. Again, tap his paws, give him the "no" command, and place him on the floor. And this time your double patience will be severely tested, for once he learns that the sofa is off limits, he'll probably try to claim residential rights to several chairs and a couple of beds. So the lesson may have to be repeated many times until he learns finally that floor level is the level for him. If tapping the paws fails to impress, slap him over the buttock with a fly swatter. It won't hurt him.

Once he knows punishment is coming, he'll stay off the furniture. Or at least he'll remain on the rug as long as you and your family are around. He won't think there's anything wrong in parking himself on an easy chair when everybody in the family is absent, for cats love comfort just as much as you do. So, if he's going to be alone in the house for a few hours, put him in a safe place with a few toys. A wire pet crate is fine for this purpose.

There's an added risk, by the way, if you happen to adopt an adult stray cat. You might reason that he'll only answer nature's calls if he's outdoors and thus doesn't need any housebreaking. Well, that would be wrong human reasoning. Any old place is fine for him and the softer the better: a rug, a chair, a sofa, a bedspread. So avoid the risk and housebreak the adult stray. Oddly, since he's mature and has more brain power, it will take longer to housebreak him than a kitten.

Collar and Leash

Any kitten can be easily trained to walk on a leash, but an adult cat considers this restriction to be an outrage and will fight the training for months. So start during kittenhood.

A light, loose-fitting collar that won't slip over his head is the first requirement. Make one out of a small leather strap. Let him wear the collar two

or three minutes at a time, several times a day, until he gets used to it. On the fourth day, attach a long string or cord to the collar. The kitten will drag it around and play with it. Fine. He's becoming accustomed to it.

After a week, pick up the loose end of the cord and use it as a leash. Now take him for short walks, but for a couple of days permit him to walk in any direction and just follow him. Then try the "Fritz, come!" command plus a gentle pull on the leash. The idea now is to make him walk your way. If he fights the idea, give him a rest and try again. Remember, short sessions! Never more than five minutes.

As soon as he discovers that there's no pull on his neck when he walks along with you, he'll prove agreeable. At that point, perhaps two weeks from the time you first put the collar on his neck, he's half trained. He'll walk with you, but usually right in front of you. So shorten the leash and keep him on one side of you. The pull on the leash will keep him with you, but remember to walk slowly. For every step you take, he must take several steps.

From this point on, the author uses a thin, show leash used for showing dogs at dog shows. This leash has an adjustable loop at one end, so there's no longer any need for the collar. Most pet stores carry these.

Some owners prefer a cat harness, but this is more expensive and it must be just the right fit, so that it doesn't restrict his free movements. He can use his whole body to fight the lead, not just his neck, so harness training calls for extra double patience on your part.

What's the point of training your pet to walk on a leash? If you live in the city, it keeps him under absolute control when you take him outdoors for a bit of fresh air. When he hears sudden, strange noises, he'll want to run and hide. No matter where you live, there will be times when you will want him close at hand as you walk down a busy street or through a strange neighborhood.

Travel

Cats do not make ideal travel companions. If your pet curls up on your lap and stays put for five miles, then he may have broken the world's record for feline inactivity.

It would seem that the cat is frightenend by the rolling motion of man's machines. The wheel is beyond his comprehension, and riding makes him restless, and sometimes it frightens him. So his first journeys should always be short ones, and he should be made to feel both safe and comfortable.

This is easily done by purchasing or making a travel case. Look one over at your nearest pet store. It has a handle for your convenience, and ventilation at both ends so that your pet gets plenty of air. Some open at one end, and others open at the top. The door or lid can be fastened to keep the cat inside. The size should be just big enough for him to stand and turn around. A length of old towel does nicely as a bed.

A good case is expensive. But they are easy enough to make out of plywood, if you're handy with tools.

Or you can use a wooden or cardboard box. Hinge the wood top and strap the cardboard flaps. If a cat can get his head through an opening he can work his body through it, so make several small holes at each end for ventilation.

He won't mind taking a trip in his special crate, so long as he's not uncomfortable. Get him used to the idea that it's safe by placing him in it several times before the first trip.

Not everyone is capable of training a cat to perform tricks. Again, it takes double patience and common sense, plus faith. Faith is important. You must be willing to believe that success can be achieved, and you must disbelieve the ninety-nine people out of one hundred who tell you that it's impossible to train a cat to do tricks.

Anyone who has successfully trained a cat to walk on a leash is qualified to teach that cat tricks, and the cat himself has enough brain power to learn tricks. It should be pleasant news to learn that once he masters one trick, the cat is much more agreeable to learning more tricks.

As in his basic training, teach one trick at a time. Make sure that he has the first trick down pat before proceeding to the next one. Since his memory isn't too strong, review the tricks he's learned every few days.

Timing is important. The incentive-reward or tidbit method of training is used, so the sessions should always be held before a regular meal. The cat can't be tempted by a favorite tidbit if he's not hungry.

For best results, the tidbits (a dozen per training session are enough) should be a food your cat finds irresistible. By the time he's ready to learn tricks, you'll know what that is. In the author's experience, brewer's yeast tablets and small pieces of cooked, dried liver have always proved effective. Still, your cat may prefer pieces of raw carrot. People are funny, and so are cats.

It doesn't make any difference where you do the training—indoors or out—so long as the site is familiar to the cat and there are no distractions. But put him on a leash. He'll soon learn that the lead means something is expected of him.

Now let's run through some simple tricks:

Shake Hands

Some cats will learn to shake hands without the tidbit method. Simply lift up one paw (always

the same one) as you say "Fritz, shake!" Then you
shake his paw, pet him, and tell him that he' a fine
fellow. Do this about ten times per session, hold
two sessions a day, and repeat day after day. Eventu-
ally your efforts will succeed, but by that time you
may be a nervous wreck.

The tidbit method calls for one practice session
a day. Start the same way by lifting his paw as you
say "Fritz, shake!" Then you shake his paw, give him
a tidbit, and praise him. Repeat three or four times.

Next, hold the tidbit in your fingers, permit him to
sniff it, and give the command. If he puts up his
paw, it will be a minor miracle, but accept it, shake
it, and give him the tidbit. If he doesn't put up his
paw, pick it up, shake it, and give him the tidbit
anyway. From start to finish, a dozen shakes are

enough for one day. A cat doesn't really concentrate and is easily bored. Oh, he'll watch a bird for hours, but that's his hunting instinct at work, and waiting doesn't mean concentration.

On the second day, and every day thereafter, start with the tidbit in your fingers. By the end of the week, he'll be shaking hands on command. From then on, you won't have to give him a tidbit every time. A pat and a few congratulatory words will do.

Roll Over

The average cat loves to lie on his back and have his belly rubbed. This amounts to half a roll. Whenever you rub his belly, give the command "Fritz, roll over!" and push him so that he completes the roll. Congratulate him. Repeat this a few hundred or thousand times, whichever is necessary, and he'll learn the trick.

You can teach him to obey the command in four or five days by using tidbits as rewards. Just be sure that he knows the tidbit is in your fingers. This is one of the easiest tricks to teach.

Up

You want him to jump up on a chair. Let him sniff the tidbit, let him see you place the tidbit on the chair seat, and then give the command "Fritz, up!" If he doesn't jump up, repeat the command as you lift him onto the chair and permit him to eat the tidbit. Praise him and put him back on the floor. Cats like to jump, and the average one learns this trick in a few days.

Since they like to jump down as well as up, this trick can be extended by placing one tidbit on the chair and a second on the floor. Then it's up onto the chair on the command "Fritz, up!" and down to the floor on the command "Fritz, down." You might have a little trouble with this one, and perhaps you'll have to lift him down from the chair to the second tidbit in the early stages of the training. And he may want to lunge for the second tidbit before jumping up for the first one—use the leash to restrain and correct him.

Once you have him going up and down, start neglecting to put the tidbit on the chair every time. He'll still jump up, but find his reward isn't there and jump down for it. At this training stage, one of the author's cats used to jump back up on the chair, as if to double check and make sure he hadn't overlooked his first tidbit. He was then given (by hand) the missing tidbit. To fit his own talents, the command was changed to "Fritz, up-down-up," and— to the amazement of many cat lovers—he performed this trick for the rest of his life. So there are times when a command can be tailored to fit an action that the cat is going to perform anyway.

Up a Ladder

This is a variation of the up theme, and the ladder is a stepladder. Start by placing the tidbit on the second step and lifting him to it until he climbs of his own accord on the command "Fritz, ladder!" If he tries to outtrick you on this by not climbing two steps and reaching out for the tidbit, outtrick him by placing the reward on the third step.

In each training session, he'll climb higher and higher. Just be sure that the stepladder stands firmly and doesn't shake when he starts to climb toward the top.

Once he gets to the top and eats his tidbit, chances are that he'll just sit there and wonder what to do next. Outdoors, he can usually be taught to jump to the ground. Indoors, he may resist the idea. But indoors or out, don't overdo the trick by using a giant sized stepladder. Eight steps is about the maximum, and start him on one with fewer steps if you have one. A three or four step kitchen ladder is ideal at the beginning.

Sit Up

Start the cat in a sitting position. Hold the tidbit over his head and just out of his reach. "Fritz, sit up!" is the command. After a few tries, he'll sit up and rest both paws on your hands. He's on his way.

If he makes a mistake and rears up full length from his hind legs, take advantage of the mistake later by holding the tidbit higher and commanding "Fritz, walk." But for this trick, don't expect too much. A cat won't take more than three or four steps.

From the sitting position, too, you can train him to respond to "Fritz, down!" Help him get the idea by holding the tidbit in one hand as you lift his front paws a little. When he's down, give him the tidbit.

With the tidbit method and double patience, the average cat can be taught any number of simple tricks. But repetition always remains important, for he has that short memory. And once he has a trick down pat, the tidbit won't be necessary every time, just once in awhile, to keep up his hopes.

Five months is early enough to start teaching tricks. As a general rule, cats make better students than kittens, and neutered cats are the easiest to train. If not neutered, the female is easier to train than the male. Even an expert will have trouble with a tom-cat, as Hollywood discovered a long time ago. Whenever you see a trick cat performing in films, you can be sure the trickster is a lady.

Can a cat be taught any practical tricks? Yes. Several of the author's dogs were trained to ring a doorbell whenever they wanted to come into the house. It was a special doorbell: a three-foot length of girth strap with pony bells attached, and the strap was hung outside the front door. By pushing the strap with their noses, or slapping it with one paw, the dogs caused the bells to ring. After watching the dogs do this for several months, one of the cats tried it. When somebody opened the front door, the cat knew he was a success. He may have been the original copycat.

He taught himself, of course, but he could have been taught by the tidbit method. If you can find some small bells, string them together, hang them on a hook, and teach your cat to be a bell ringer. Of course, if he likes the music of the bells, he may decide to ring them at any hour of the day or night.

VII.

the pink of condition

The discouraging thing about the pet cat is that so many things can go wrong with him. On the brighter side, the cat builds up immunity to many illnesses as he ages, and most go through life in reasonably healthy fashion. Veterinarians are thankful for that, for there aren't enough of them to see every cat once a year, not even if they worked twenty-four hours a day.

A quartet of telltale signs signify a sick cat. He may display one, several, or all of them:

1) Coat: dull, uneven, dry to the touch.

2) Eyes: runny, discharging, or presence of third lid.

3) Actions: avoiding people, hiding, loss of appetite with excessive drinking.

4) Temperature: deviating from normal, or 101.5°F. The bigger the deviation, the sicker the cat. Thus, at 99°F or 103°F, drop everything and rush him to the vet.

The only instrument you'll need for checking out all four signs, of course, is a thermometer. Place your pet in standing position, hold him there (you'll probably need help) and insert thermometer one inch into his rectum. Hold it there for three minutes, then remove and read. A rectal thermometer is best.

The kitten or cat who displays all four signs is in serious trouble. Chances are that he's also vomiting and has diarrhea. The strong probability is that he has either feline enteritis or pneumonitis. Now it's too late for the preventive vaccines, but not too late to dash for the vet. Don't wait.

Those are the two commonest and dangerous diseases, and unless you invest in those *preventitive shots,* you run the risk of losing your pet. They strike kittens and cats of any age.

Aside from those two diseases, many of the common ailments and illnesses can be diagnosed and treated at home. Indeed, many of the ills can be avoided by just keeping your eyes open for such cat enemies as:

Fleas

Cat fleas come in two sizes: tiny hoppers (males) and bigger crawlers (females). Both sexes are blood suckers and cause tapeworms, heartworms, skin diseases, loss of weight, and poor coats. Enough of them can kill a cat, so they're no laughing matter. A dull coat and excessive scratching are sure signs of fleas. One of the benefits of regular grooming is that you'll notice their presence. Cure by rubbing cat flea powder into his coat and right down to the

skin. Brush out after twenty minutes. Repeat performance one week later. But that's only half the story,
for flea eggs will have dropped from the cat's coat.
So clean out his sleeping quarters, powder, and replace old bedding with new.

Lice

A cat infested with lice scratches more than a
cat with fleas. They are biters as well as blood
suckers, and also killers. They live only a few days,
but eggs hatch right in the cat's coat, so a new

generation is always coming along. Skin diseases, loss of weight, and anemia are the result. Cure by applying cat lice powder to coat and rubbing it in. Brush out after thirty minutes. Repeat for three days, wait ten days, repeat for three more days.

Mites

If you suspect that your cat has fleas or lice and can't find any, then he probably has mites. There are many kinds, all so small that they can't be seen by the naked eye. If the cat scratches his ears and shakes his head, he probably has ear mites. They are the causes of mange, scabies, and tumors. They are blood suckers and dangerous. There's no effective home cure. See your vet.

Ticks

Not a problem in some areas of the country, but you can't miss a tick when you're grooming. They burrow into the skin and suck blood until bloated, and then they're very easy to see. Ticks spread a number of common diseases and weaken the cat. Remove them by soaking a piece of cotton in rubbing alcohol. Pinch the cotton over tick for one minute. Then use tweezers or fingers to pull out tick. Be sure you get tick's head, for it will cause infection. And be sure to kill the tick. If your area is full of ticks, effective coat rinses are available. Applied to cat's coat, these rinses discourage ticks from joining the cat.

Worms

Most kittens have worms, and so do most cats who haven't been dewormed since kittenhood. *Felis catus* can play host to quite a variety: such common ones as round worms, hook worms, and tape worms; such special ones as muscle, eye, heart, and stomach worms. All are bad for him, for they weaken him and lessen his immunity to many diseases. Some cause their own disease. A skinny cat, nervous, with a pot belly and irregular eating habits is a sure carrier of worms.

There are many home cures on the market for worms, but the trick is to know which type of worm or worms to treat. Your vet will know.

Ringworm

This common skin disease is caused by a fungus, not a worm. It is highly contagious, and can spread from the infected cat to all other animals, including man. It looks like an irregular, red oval on skin, and usually apears first on ears, face or neck. Bald spots result. Ringworm is easily cured at home, but under vet's instructions.

Rickets

The kitten who has trouble walking, or seems lame (if he hasn't had an accident), or drags his rear legs has rickets. This really means that his bones are soft and are not developing properly, and in turn this means that his diet is deficient. He's not getting enough calcium and vitamin D.

Supplement his meals with calcium and vitamin D foods or powders. On the advice of English friends, the author has always added one-half tablet of brewer's yeast, three time weekly, to regular kitten diets. None of the kittens has ever suffered from rickets.

Anemia

Overall, the cat appears listless. He doesn't eat, loses weight, rests continually, and may try to vomit. Too many lice, hookworms, or not enough iron and copper in his diet may be the causes. Anemia has many varieties, but all can be cured by the expert—if caught in time. So, consult the vet.

Hair Balls

This is one of the cat's penalties for keeping himself so clean. Some of his coat hairs cling to his rough-surfaced tongue, and he swallows those hairs. The hairs join together in an internal mass of irregular shape, but it's called a hair ball. It causes constipation. The cat tries to get rid of the ball by coughing it up. Sometimes he succeeds, but he almost chokes in the process. Regular grooming cuts down on the dead hairs in his coat, but you can't remove all of them for him. Add a half teaspoon of mineral oil to his meals twice a week, and that will oil the hair balls for easy passage through his innards. Or do as the author does and smear a little plain petroleum jelly on his nose twice a week. He'll lick this off and swallow it, and the jelly will grease the hair balls.

Poisons

Every minute counts when the cat swallows poison. He must get rid of the poison, and he can't do it by himself. You must help him by forcing him to swallow a liquid that will make him regurgitate and vomit the poison. It's a good idea to have hydrogen peroxide on hand in your medicine cabinet at all times, just in case. Mix it with equal amounts of water (50-50) before giving to cat. And it's also a good idea to have at least a rough estimate of your kitten's or cat's weight at all times. The proper dosage is one teaspoonful for every two pounds of cat weight.

The cat should empty the poison within three minutes. Then phone your vet. Tell him, if you know, the poison your cat swallowed, and describe the symptoms to him (pain, foamy mouth, convulsions, panting, coma).

If the moment of poisoning arrives and you can't find the hydrogen peroxide, use plain vinegar or plain lemon juice. One tablespoon for every three pounds of cat. Then phone your vet.

Diarrhea

Spoiled food, change of diet, wrong diet, and too large chunks of food may cause diarrhea. The treatment is simple enough, but if the condition doesn't clear up in a couple of days, then it's wise to see the vet. Diarrhea, by itself, is nothing to worry about. But if it persists, remember that it's a symptom of many serious diseases. A half teaspoon of Kaopectate usually does the trick. Some cats hate it, some lick it from the spoon, others take it in their food. Repeat on second day if condition persists. When successful, feed small meals for a couple of days. Don't repeat on third day. Something else is wrong with your cat if he still has diarrhea.

Common Cold

Sure, the cat can catch a cold, just as you do. He suffers, but not much, from a runny nose, watery eyes, and sneezing.

Rest, and a baby aspirin twice a day, send the average cat cold away. Not right away, but in two or three days.

Cuts, Scratches, Bruises

If they are minor, treat them the same as you would your own, and the cat's healing tongue will do the rest. A severe cut or wound, of course, always means the vet. Until you can get to his office, the problem will probably be stopping the cat's loss of blood. Apply a wad of cotton or a small, clean sponge and then apply a pressure bandage, and don't worry. It's a rare cat who bleeds to death.

Fits

Worms, teething, fright, excitement, and exhaustion are the major causes of fits. Cats aren't often troubled, but kittens are. A mild fit, such as dashing about in panic, isn't cause for alarm. Find the cause and get rid of it. One fit doesn't necessarily mean that the kitten will have another.

Symptoms of serious fits include frothing at the mouth, unconsciousness, a body so rigid that the kitten falls, thrashing of legs, bumping into things, and shrieks of pain. Mild or serious, don't go near the kitten until the fit has run its course. Then pick him up by the scruff of the neck—he won't feel the pain—so that he can't bite you, put him in a dark place, and keep him quiet. A couple of mild fits or one serious fit amount to trouble. Until you can get him to the vet, give him a baby aspirin and provide fresh water, but no food.

Rabies

This is one of the oldest diseases known to man, but it's still fatal most of the time. It is usually transmitted through the bites of rabid dogs, skunks, foxes, rats, and bats. It takes a couple of weeks for the infected cat to show any symptoms. Then he undergoes a complete change of personality, he cries often in a hoarse voice, and he may try to hide from the world or attack every living thing in sight, including you. And a rabid cat can infect you. There's nothing you can do. Consult your vet and follow his advice. If you live in the suburbs or country, a vaccine immunizing the healthy cat against rabies is available and is a wise investment. Fortunately, the disease is now rare among dogs, rarer among cats.

Unless your pet cat was born under a very lucky star, he's going to run into one or more of the foregoing difficulties somewhere along the line. Unless you know something about handling an ailing cat, you are going to have difficulty attempting to treat him. A gentle, lovable kitten may turn into a stubborn, biting, scratching wild animal when you try to give him something for his own good. He just doesn't understand, and he feels awful anyway.

Giving him medicine or a tablet is really a two-person job. Wrap the kitten in a towel so that all four legs are immobile and his head is free. Hold the patient in firm fashion. If your assistant is the holder, have him sit down with the patient on his lap.

Now, if you're giving him a tablet, place your left hand over the cat's head, pull the head back until the nose is up, and press on either side of the upper jaw with thumb and one finger. With other hand, pull lower jaw down until mouth is wide open, then pop tablet as far back over tongue as possible. Permit cat to close mouth. If he spits out the tablet, repeat until he swallows it. You can be stubborn, too.

To give liquid medicine, tilt back his head. Where his lips join, press in on the upper lip and pull out on the lower until a pocket is formed. Pour the medicine into this pocket. Pour slowly and a little at a time. He may spit some of it out, but he'll swallow most of it.

The wrapped towel method is best for most first aid moments. In case of a cut paw, for example, just leave the leg belonging to that paw exposed for treatment.

And it will be a case of not one towel but many on the day that your kitten or cat decides to tangle with a skunk. The traditional method for removing the skunk odor from the victim's coat is to bathe the victim in tomato juice. But this takes many baths, and in the end the cat smells like tomato juice.

Less expensive, and far less trouble, is a warm water bath. Use a liquid coconut oil base soap. Work soap lather right down to the skin. The more you work, the more effective the bath. Rinse with clean, warm water. Rub dry, and be sure to comb and brush the dead hairs from the coat. If a faint odor remains, that means a second bath. Warm water, by the way, doesn't mean scalding water. And two people are always better than one for this job, if you are fortunate enough to have a willing friend. And if it's any help, you will never have to go through the same process again. Not with the same cat, anyway. He has that much intelligence.

VIII.
myths about cats

"A falling cat always lands on his feet."

Often, but not always, and if the distance is great enough, the cat can break every leg. Accidental cat deaths in the United States rate this way: (1) falling, (2) hit by car, (3) poisoning. Cats love to perch on window sills, and if your pet lives above the first floor, it's wise to install screens or protective guards around open windows.

"Cats need milk."

Kittens, yes, but not cats. Many adults can't be forced to drink milk. But the cat can't function without water (70% of his body weight), so fresh water should always be available for him.

"A wormed cat never acquires worms again."

He doesn't brag about it, but the cat plays host to more types of worms than most other animals. At least an annual checkup at the vet's should be part of his life program.

"All calico *cats are females."*

A male calico is rare, but he does occur. To date, all have been *sterile.*

"Cats don't shed."

They shed continually, but more in summer than winter. It's a matter of light. The more the daylight, the more the shedding.

"Neutered cats become fat and lazy."

Fat cats are spoiled, overfed brats who don't get enough exercise. Normally, the only side effect of neutering is a slightly denser coat.

"Cats shouldn't eat fruits."

Any fruit, fresh or canned, that won't harm you, won't harm your cat. However, it boils down to a matter of individual taste buds. Some cats love fruit and others hate it.

"A swimming cat is unusual."

All cats are capable of swimming, and many do every day of the week.

"The black cat is unlucky."

Only if you believe that a Friday the 13th is an unlucky day.

"A purring cat is a happy, contented cat."

Not always, and not all cats purr. Those that do have
a variety to express such emotions as pleasure,
anxiety and pain. Cat language also includes a variety
of mews, chats, hisses, growls, shrieks, and screams.
While he cannot roar, thank heaven, the cat as a
maker of sounds ranks third among all animals. Man
and the monkey are his only superiors.

"All cats are mice killers."

Most are, and the talent will develop as early as four
months of age. It's claimed, and it's probably true,
that no two cats are ever precisely alike. So there are
many cats who won't go after mice, and some cats
who are frightened by the little rodents, and still
others who regard mice as playmates.

*"Cats never need baths, for they keep themselves
clean."*

Yes, they are clean animals, but they'll still come
home with coats full of mud, coal dust, and smelly
substances. When that happens, wet the entire coat
with warm water, then work a lather of soft soap right
down to the skin. Rinse, make sure all soap is removed, and repeat if necessary. Sometimes, as in
cases of paint, stains, oils, and tar, kerosene is the
answer. Just rub hairs with kerosene until they are
clean. Then follow with a soap and water bath until
all the kerosene has been removed.

"A white cat is a deaf cat."

Often true in the case of the blue-eyed white. Not true in the case of the pink-eyed (albino), green-eyed, or yellow-eyed.

"A caterwauling cat means that somebody nearby is dying."

The same thing is said about a howling dog, and both sayings are nonsense. The weird, high pitched caterwaul is the cat's song. Just one of the many sounds he makes, but the only one he utters with head held back and nose up.

"A cat never touches an alcoholic drink."

Don't bet on it. Those that do imbibe always show the after effects. However, cats don't smoke.

"A cat can catch distemper from a dog."

No, nor can a dog catch distemper from a cat. To each his own. Cat distemper has been mentioned before under one of its other names: feline infectious enteritis.

"Cats and dogs are natural enemies."

It seems that way, but use some common sense and double patience in introducing a cat to a dog and there's seldom any trouble. Because of his superior reflexes and the way he's built, the average cat—if he really wants to—will defeat the average dog in a fight. But the average cat prefers peace.

"The cat is the only animal who will look you in the eye."

This is a common claim of cat lovers who somehow read honesty into such a feat. But a gorilla will do the same thing, and so will a dog when he wants to eat something that you're eating.

"A cat has nine lives."

Only true in the case of nine cats. The myth really started as a compliment, and it meant that the cat had an amazing talent for squirming out of a dangerous situation.

"Cats smother sleeping human babies by sucking their breath."

Believe it or not, this is still believed by some super-stitious people. *Ailurophobes,* mostly.

"A calico cat is worth a fortune."

A modern myth that has been around for less than twenty years. It seems that some branch of the federal government involved in research will pay ten thousand dollars for a calico cat. Calico is the most difficult coat color to achieve in breeding, but there will always be calico cats around. The only big problem is finding the federal agency.

"A kitten may have more than one sire."

Just one sire per kitten, but each kitten in a given litter can have a different sire. That happens when the queen cat is permitted to mate at will. In such cases, it's not unusual for her to mate again in a few weeks, and then she is double-pregnant and carries two litters. So three weeks after the first *kittening,* a second litter is born. Now the queen needs help feeding her *kendle.* And people complain about rabbits!

"The skunk and the cat belong to the same family tree."

No, the skunk belongs to the weasel family and is a cousin of the otter and mink.

"Pull on their tails to break up a cat fight."

Never touch a fighting cat! Not even your own beloved pet! In the excitement, he's sure to turn on you. Turn a hose on the battlers, or toss a pail of water over them, or create the biggest noise you can think of. And always stay a good ten feet away from the cats.

"A bell on his collar prevents a cat from catching songbirds."

Not for long. The bird hunter soons learns how to overcome the bell by timing his jumping. If your cat is a bird hunter and this fact bothers you, keep him indoors—at least during the nesting season.

glossary

Adult	over eight months
Ailurophile	cat lover
Ailurophobe	cat hater
Altering	operation to make male cat impotent
Calico	coat color combination of black, red, cream and white
Calling	female's mating call
Caterwaul	cat's howl
Cat fancy	the world of serious cat lovers: breeders and owners of purebreds who make cat shows possible
Cattery	home for cats
Clowder	group of cats
Dam	female parent
Domestic	tame
Exotic	wild, and usually of foreign origin
Feral	wild, but from domestic stock
Glove	patch of color over paw
Hybrid	a breed resulting from a cross of other breeds
Kendle	group of kittens
Kibble	small chunks of dry, granular pet food
Kitten	under eight months
Kittening	birthing

Lace	patch of color coming to a point or points
Litter	family of kittens
Mauve	shade of violet
Neutering	operations to make cats un-breedable
Points	the ears, mask, legs and tail
Preventive shots	inoculations to guard a kitten or cat against these serious diseases: feline enteritis (similar to distemper); pneumonitis (virus infection); rabies (brain inflammation). First two are musts
Queen	mother cat
Retractable	capable of being withdrawn
Selective breeding	science of breeding based on the laws of inheritance
Sire	male parent
Spaying	operation to make female cat unbreedable
Sport	a variation, not usual
Spray	male's urine
Standard	man's definition of the perfect cat
Sterile	not capable of breeding
Tabby	coat with pattern of stripes
Ticking	specks of color on coat
Tomcat	adult male capable of breeding
Weaning	period when kitten learns to exist on foods other than own mother's milk
Whole	physically entire or normal, thus not neutered

ANATOMY OF THE CAT

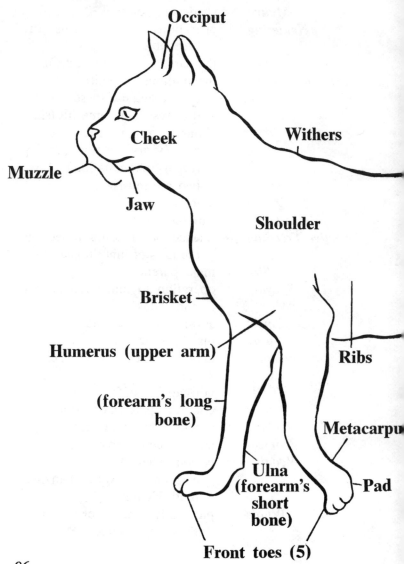

Occiput

Cheek

Withers

Muzzle

Jaw

Shoulder

Brisket

Humerus (upper arm)

Ribs

(forearm's long bone)

Metacarpu

Ulna
(forearm's
short
bone)

Pad

Front toes (5)

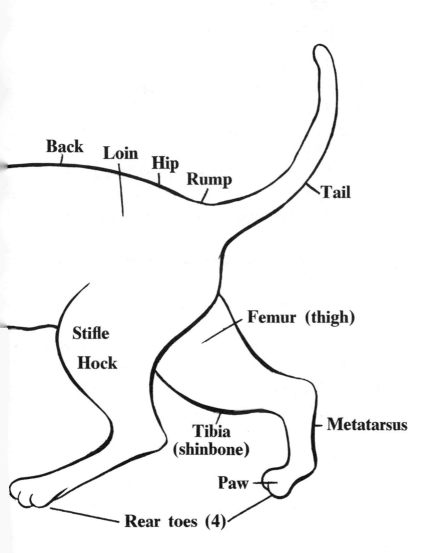

Back
Loin
Hip
Rump
Tail
Stifle
Hock
Femur (thigh)
Tibia
(shinbone)
Metatarsus
Paw
Rear toes (4)

CATDOM'S GOVERNING BODIES

Write the Secretary of the association or federation nearest you for information concerning membership, clubs, shows, recognized breeds and standards, and breeders:

American Cat Association, 11366 Camaloa Ave., Lakeview Terrace, Calif. 91342

American Cat Fanciers Association, Box 3637, Austin, Texas 78704

Canadian Cat Association, 41 Victoria St., London, Ontario, Canada.

Cat Fanciers Association, Box 430, Red Bank, N.J. 07701

Cat Fanciers Federation, 629 Kutcher Road, Southampton, Pa. 18966

Crown Cat Fanciers Association, Rt. 3, Box 347½, Huntsville, Al. 35806

National Cat Fanciers Association, 8219 Rosemont Ave., Detroit, Mich. 48228

United Cat Federation, 2202 Morose St., Lemon Grove, Calif. 92045

HOME READING

Of many publications devoted to cats, these two are the best of the lot and can be found at most libraries:

Cats Magazine (2900 Jefferson Ave., Washington, Pa. 15301), a monthly with news, pictures, tips, calendar of show dates and places, and listing of leading breeders.

Cat Fancy (488 Madison Ave., New York, N.Y. 10022), a bimonthly with informative articles, short fiction, and full color art worthy of framing.

index